Stonelight

For Kevin Perryman,
and in memory of our friend

Sheenagh Pugh
Stonelight

seren

seren
is the book imprint of
Poetry Wales Press Ltd
Wyndham Street, Bridgend, Wales

The right of Sheenagh Pugh to be identified as the
Author of this Work has been asserted in accordance with
the Copyright, Designs and Patents Act, 1988

© Sheenagh Pugh, 1999

ISBN 1-85411-243-0

A CIP record for this title is available from
the British Library

All rights reserved. No part of this publication may be reproduced,
stored in a retrieval system, or transmitted at any time or by any means
electronic, mechanical, photocopying, recording or otherwise
without the prior permission of the copyright holder.

*The publisher acknowledges the financial assistance of the
Arts Council of Wales*

Cover photograph: Sam Burns

Printed in Palatino by WBC Book Manufacturers, Bridgend

Contents

7	Stonelight
8	The Beachcomber
9	The Arctic Chart
9	I. The Parry Islands
11	II. Fury Beach
12	III. Kane Basin
13	IV. Bellot Strait
15	V. M'Clintock Channel
16	VI. Lady Franklin Bay
18	Stylist: Senior Perms
20	Bolshies
21	Envying Owen Beattie
23	Fluent
24	What's wrong with perfection anyway?
25	Graffiti Man
27	The Faithful Wife
28	Cigarette Smoke
29	New Made
31	Red Helmet
32	Love Song
33	Goodnight
34	Together
35	Ikon
36	Postcard
37	Rather
38	It's Only Love
39	And when I got there
40	The Treasure-House
41	Far Places
43	The Garden
44	Ronas Hill
45	As If

46 Letter
47 The Tormented Censor
48 Bryn Asaph
50 Aardvark
51 The City of Empty Rooms
52 Pause: Rewind
54 Unkindness
55 Crossing the Bridge
57 The Comet-Watcher's Perspective
58 Tutorial

TRANSLATIONS

61 Simon Dach
 (May the bond of friendship always be
 held in honour)
63 Andreas Gryphius
 (Midday)
64 Christian Hofmann von Hofmannswaldau
 (To Fleur)
65 Paul Fleming
 (For a young lady, to send to her sweetheart)
66 (On remembering his first girlfriend)
67 (For her sake)
68 Christine de Pisan
 (If I'm in church every day)
69 (Of all the lilies of the field)
70 (To sing a happy song with a sad heart)

71 *Notes*
72 *Acknowledgements*

Stonelight

"Not the frailest thing in creation can ever be lost"
— George Mackay Brown

Each stone happens
in its own way. One stands
true in a house-wall.

Anger quickens another: it flies,
fills a mouth with blood.

Shaped and polished, one shines
in the eyes of many.

One seems inert, earth-embedded:
underneath, colonies are teeming.

But the best are seal-smooth,
and the hand that chose them

sends them skimming, once, twice,
ten times over the ocean, to the edge

of sight, and whenever they brush the water's skin,
an instant is bruised

into brightness. The eye flinches. When they sink,
if they sink, the light they left

wells out, spills, seeds itself, prickling
like stars, on a field that never takes
the same shape twice.

The Beachcomber

i.m. George Mackay Brown

At the edges of every man,
a flotsam of stories.

They come in on the currents
that circle the world

carrying driftwood and history,
love-songs and plastic bottles.

They are scabbed with rust, scarred
all over by the salt of travel;

most men leave them lie. It takes
keen eyes to spot, among dulse

and wrack, the sudden gleam
of nacre; the blackened silver:

sharp ears to catch, above talk
and traffic, the ghost of a song.

The Arctic Chart

*"There is nothing worth living for, but to have
one's name inscribed on the Arctic chart."*
— Alfred, Lord Tennyson

I

The Parry Islands

Winter man, first of your kind
to sail that great sound with its chain
of islands, scattering names

from home: Devon, Somerset,
Cornwallis, Melville. First to spend
long months of darkness

in an empty land. The snow
stretched so flat, distance
lost all meaning;

the eye strained for a mark.
You learned the world *cold*
in a new language:

the tongue locked fast
to a man's beard; the scald of metal
on flesh. Mercury swelled;

shattered thermometers. Steam froze
on the ovens. But you had looked,
from a mountain, out over

the drifting distorted towers
shivering light,
and sensed behind them

an immense mind, unexplored,
unbounded; you could never chart it,
though you knew its name.

Edward Parry: believer, searcher,
living in awe; more humbled
by each new wonder.

II

Fury Beach

On the barest of beaches, open to the gales
that drove her aground, they left her: all her crew
crammed in her sister-ship, looking back, anguished,
sick with the failure

of losing a ship. The luck had never been with them:
they had found nowhere; had nothing to show
for their journey north. Their captain was going home
to a court-martial,

and *Fury* was lost, broken on the beach.
How could they know, defeat stinging their eyes,
her name would become a landmark for starving men?
How many stranded explorers

made for that beach where a ship's stores lay heaped,
food in the wasteland, boats to escape the ice;
how many saw through tears their lives given back;
how many men went home?

HMS *Fury*: built in Napoleon's time,
driven ashore by a gale on Somerset Island,
lost and then found, again and again: life-saver,
wrecked on a lucky day.

III

Kane Basin

Dead man running round the world, chasing
all the life you could get, one beat ahead
of your leaky, racing heart. Never pausing

at books or music: barely time to read
the world through your eyes, let alone another's.
A day without something new was wasted —

it might have been the last. The pretty manners
of your boyhood, left behind in your wake;
a comet's tail of casual hurts, sharp answers:

you weren't good at people. They take
too long: you'd other things to think about.
When you saw the winter ice break

with a great, rippling wave, like a carpet
shaken out: when you heard the bergs grind
like rasping sugar, you were sensing it

with a rush of blood; with every nerve-end.
Of all the drugs you'd studied, the most potent
was the world you'd have to leave behind

before you were old. Driven, impatient,
arrogant: all that, and small wonder.
I doubt I could have stood you a moment,

Elisha Kent Kane: doctor, explorer,
poser, pain in the neck. My life has lasted
longer than yours already, and I will never
live half as much, dead man, as you did.

IV

Bellot Strait

Little Bellot,
they called you:
the home town
that paid your way
through college; the widow
you went to help
in another country,
who spoke of you
as her own son.

Wherever you travelled,
you saw brothers,
and so there were.
Your sledge crew wrapped
ox-hides around you
while you were sleeping;
the Inuit, hardened
to kinfolk's death,
cried over yours.

You'd gone beyond
one land, one race,
calling all humans
your countrymen.
At ease among strangers
with a common cause,
you dreamed of nations
coming together
as men had done.

Joseph-René Bellot:
French officer, citizen
of the world;
it was not your heart,
nor your unfenced soul,
that caused a friend
to choose for you
the smallest strait
in the Arctic.

V

M'Clintock Channel

It grinds down from the Beaufort Sea, slow
as old men's jaws: a great stream of slabs
split off the ice-pack, rasping, crushing,
squeezing between the islands: Melville, Banks,
then down that wide channel east of Victoria,
a mile a month, and no ship gets past it,

—none tried, for years. They'd see the ice-stream
and look for the way back. You looked
for a way round: a narrow, untried strait
whose icebound mouth drove you back six times;
a long, aching sledge trek. You were a man
to do what you set out to,

a practical man; no dreamer. Yet you fixed
heraldic banners to your sleds; quested
at your own expense for the widow's husband;
refused her money; did what needed doing
as no-one else had. A man of deeds,
not words. Your words came slow

and plain: when you found the poor bones
bare in the snow; the abandoned luggage,
you hung no colours to your sentences.
"They fell down and died as they walked along."
Leopold M'Clintock: prosaic knight-errant;
man of few words, every one exact.

VI

Lady Franklin Bay

It lies in the north, lady,
where you never came,
in the white, locked world where you never
could follow him.

You went to the outer isles
at the country's end,
to ask all the homebound whalers
news of your husband.

*As you came through the Davis Strait,
down from Baffin Bay,
did you hear nothing of my love,
who had passed that way?*

You sent out your freelance captains,
Forsyth and Snow,
Inglefield, Kennedy, M'Clintock,
little Bellot,

to seek him; and every ship
took your thoughts with her.
The lie of that land; its ice,
its waters, its winter,

were all your study, as if
you could never know
enough of the place he was in,
or what he went through.

Each channel, each strait on his way,
you could have charted.
—Oh lady, you were a widow
before your search started.

He lies in the north, lady,
where your heart came:
nothing belongs up there
so much as your name.

Stylist: Senior Perms

She can do you a cut-and-blow-dry
as well as the next girl,
but she saves all her skill
for the Perms. Forget trimming a fringe:
this is God, this is mastery;
this is a challenge.

The little old ladies slip in
with their hair so lank
and so thin; so much pink
gaping though. They ask for the hair
of girlhood, that won't come again,
but she can do better.

Their colourless hanks will take shades
too subtle for girls.
The gold in the champagne bubbles,
quartz-rose and impossible blue
tint their tired heads,
and she smiles, as artists do,

then combs in the viscous magic
that thickens each strand,
and carefully sculpts it around
the curlers. Then under the dryer
for ages, but they're laid-back;
they weren't going anywhere.

You wouldn't believe all the height
she can add; all the volume
she spins with a back-comb.
When she's done, the scalp's lost in candyfloss,
frozen waves, starlight,
morning through glass.

And they walk out, heads held so high,
and sass back the roofers
for whistling.... I hope she insures
her hands, like a great violinist:
it's something, to tease out beauty
as well as this stylist.

Bolshies

In the last days of a lost war,
a man occupying a Brussels office
made time for spite; signed an order
to send one final trainload down the line
to the death camps. And his secretary
typed it, and a clerk bespoke the train,
and policemen who had no heart for the job
loaded the prisoners anyway.

But then it was all down to the lads
on the line: the drivers, the signalmen,
the track gangs, and all of a sudden
points seized up; urgent repairs took days,
you couldn't lay your hands on spare parts.
Wrong-set signals sent the train trundling
in circles while the bolshie branch rep
wheeled out his trusty, well-oiled excuses.

And when peace finally turned up
ahead of the spare parts; when the prisoners
could all change trains, and the bosses commenced
awarding themselves medals, the lads went back
to looking out for each other, fiddling time-sheets,
arguing over demarcation lines,
doing their best to baulk each jack-in-office
who tried to make the trains run on time.

Envying Owen Beattie

To have stood on the Arctic island
by the graves where Franklin's men
buried their shipmates: good enough.

To hack through the permafrost
to the coffin, its loving plaque
cut from a tin can: better.

And freeing the lid; seeing
the young sailor cocooned in ice,
asleep in his glass case.

Then melting it so gently, inch
by inch, a hundred years
and more falling away, all the distance

of death a soft hiss of steam
on the air, till at last they cupped
two feet, bare and perfect,

in their hands, and choked up,
because it was any feet
poking out of the bedclothes.

And when the calm, pinched
twenty-year-old face
came free, and he lay there,

five foot four of authentic
Victorian adventurer, tuberculous,
malnourished: John Torrington

the stoker, who came so far
in the cold, and someone whispered:
It's like he's unconscious.

Then Beattie stooped; lifted him
out of bed, the six stone
limp in his arms, and the head lolled

and rested on his shoulder,
and he felt the rush
that reckless trust sends

through parents and lovers. To have him
like that; the frail, diseased
little time-traveller;

to feel the lashes prickle
your cheek; to be that close
to the parted lips:

you would know all the fairy-tales
spoke true: how could you not try
to wake him with a kiss?

Fluent

The current of this man's talk
snags sometimes. Slams into boulders.
Stutters to a halt in a dam
of autumn debris. We wait. Wanting
to help. Knowing he'd hate it.
Watching his mouth shape, over
and over, the same word.
Breathing out, when at last
the locked sound bursts through.

Later, I'll read his poems and ride
the big wave; rock like a rowing-boat
on the sure, inevitable swell
of his flooding words.

What's wrong with perfection anyway?

It's spring again, time for the nation's press
to have a go at you. "The man has won
too often; he's too good at what he does.
He never looks like missing; where's the fun
in that? An iceberg, an automaton...."
The hate-mail throws up some, I've heard it said,
who want to see you lose, or see you dead.

Now, I am fond of losers — after all,
I am one — and they have their legends too.
I warm to Wallenstein and Hannibal,
Spartacus, Jimmy White, and all the crew
of classy guys who would have made it through
with fewer late nights or a bit more nous;
who blew it all by being too like us.

That's human, and must touch a human heart.
And yet it's no less human that a man,
now and again, is master of his art
so much, that those who watch him will breathe in
with fear, because they've seen perfection.
But there's no thunderbolt; it never was
great gods, but small men, who were envious.

And I don't need you to be fallible,
any more than I'd want my money back
because the tenor in the concert hall
never hit a duff note. I can take
genius, without complaining of a lack
of tension: in fact, it's all I want.
I love to watch you doing what I can't,

reaching so far, moving so fluently,
assurance glowing off you, like the light
off a snowfield. As I love to see
a handsomer face than mine in the street,
or hum a tune I don't know how to write.
Three sights to lift the heart: the northern sun;
barley under the wind; something well done.

Graffiti Man

Flint scratched a stick-man
into stone: *me*. A wavy spear
perched on its hand: *me hunting*.

He torched his way across continents,
Als'kander, Iskandar, Sikandar,
founding Alexandrias.

He wrote his name on diseases,
roses and children; scribbled it in neon
across skyscrapers;

spiked programs with its virus.
He sprayed it on ohms, sandwiches,
wellingtons, dahlias, hoovers.

White columns, grey stones, black walls,
heavy with names beyond number.
Such a one died

in war; of AIDS; from old age.
I, Kallaischros, lie
in the restless sea,

no-one knows where, and this stone
lies too, marking the place
where I am not.

Leningrad's gone, and Rhodesia,
scrubbed off the stone.
Ideas are harder

to clean: names won't come loose
from a phrase of music,
a story, a law, a faith,

but you need a keen edge
to carve them. Most settle
for a can of spray-paint.

On every stretch of sand
stick-swirled patterns,
waiting for the tide;

on every snowfield
the definition of footprints,
crumbling in the sun;

on every window
words, fading on the brief
page of mist.

Segunders are named each day,
and if you breathe on the window,
the words come back.

Note: Lines 17-21 are a somewhat free adaptation of an epigram by Leonidas of Tarentum from the Greek Anthology.

The Faithful Wife

My friend was leaning on the shredder; she looked sick.
She said: "I just committed adultery".
I thought: that's a good trick, in a crowded office.
"No", she said impatiently, "in my heart.

I'd been telling myself for months it was OK,
that I loved his liveliness, his bright mind;
besides, he was gay. It would never get physical.
I just felt kindly towards him, like a mother.

And the dreams could come, no harm. I'd fantasize
him ill, and visit him; in grief, and make
him smile; dry his eyes. But even in dreams
I was never tempted to take it any further.

And then just now, he wasn't even in my thoughts,
and I heard his voice, I think he was asking the time,
and it slammed into my guts. My arms ache,
and I can't breathe for him. I can't breathe."

Cigarette Smoke

Her parents smoked; she moved away,
became an oxygen junkie. No ashtrays
in the house. Her man, coming back
from the pub Friday nights, would take
a quick shower; make sure his hair
smelt clean. And she'd comb her fingers
through it; cool her lips an instant
on sleek dampness with a faint scent.

That was then. Tobacco clings
to paper; did you know? She's fanning
a letter lightly across her face,
breathing in the nicotine, the staleness.
The taste catches her throat; flows
behind her eyes. She dreams now
of drowning her mouth in black unbrushed
hair, acrid and soft as ash.

New Made

In the train, you woke me:
Look, lambs! I swallowed
the words: *what d'you expect
in March*, because your face
was a lit window: Adam,
wondering at the whiteness
of the first lamb.

I wish you could come to Wust
with me this summer.
I could sleep my way over
the North German plain,
while your young eyes filled
with storks nesting on rooftops
and deer in the corn.

And when we get there,
they'll be having a brownout,
no post till Tuesday
and the bakery waiting
for flour, and you'll think
it's all an adventure:
you might even convince me.

I'll watch the old widows
trying to add up
your armour of ear-studs
and your shy courtesy.
I'll grin when they give back
your smile, teach you phrases,
scold you for smoking.

I'll show you the paths
lit with silver birches
for travellers through the dark.
At the young soldier's grave
I'll make your eyes
cloud over with pity,
and in the old church,

I'll ask Pastor Stephan
to lower the gilded angel
who lives in the rafters.
She comes down to christen children,
to make them new. I'll believe it,
too, when I see her mirrored
in your kindling eyes.

Red Helmet

Your hair was soot-black:
it mopped up light
and gave none back. You slipped in
and out with shadows.

You've coloured it danger,
a banner's pride.
All the shades of fire
defy your shyness.

I see you move,
far off, unmistakable.
You run your hand
through a red helmet,

and it catches the sun.
Light shivers
at your touch; breaks up,
goes all to pieces.

Love Song

If I were a bank manager
and your debts were mounting,
I'd extend your overdraft
without even counting.

If I were an examiner
and you hadn't a clue,
I'd give you the answers
and all my love, too.

If I were a shopkeeper
I'd use no lock;
you could lift my spirits,
my heart, and my stock.

If I were a constable
I'd turn a blind eye
to your stash, and smile
as the smoke wafted by.

If I were a magistrate
I'd fine you a kiss;
if I were your doctor
I'd be up for malpractice,

but if I were me
and loved you that way,
you'd never guess,
and I'd never say.

Goodnight

The worries are prowling the wood;
the moon is yellow
in their mad eyes, and they're singing,
but they won't touch you.

And I've put poison down
for the guilt that gnaws
and scurries in the skirting-boards
all through your house.

I'll stifle the steady drip
of the tasks you put off
till tomorrow: I'll soothe the night-hunger
of unfed love.

I'll watch your eyelids for dreams,
and if they come back,
I'll stroke them away. I promise
I'll stay awake.

Your lips move in sleep, counting
my wishes for you.
One thousand; one thousand and one;
one thousand and two....

Together

He looked so small, huddled
in her coat, still shivering
in a snowfall of white wool,

then, in a while, nestling
into the collar, his smile
rested on hers: that's all.

Back in the coat, she tries
to sense his smoke, his presence,
and gets no trace.

And he walks on, hugging
thin shoulders and a weight
of worries; chilled-off, alone.

Ikon

In her mind an ikon
glows: a dark-eyed face.
It was painted straight on
to the wall; if she cuts it out
now, she must take plaster
and all, and leave its shape
in the bare brick.

Postcard

Seal in the voe, dark head, I thought of you;
skuas diving on fulmars; I don't trust
your lover. Thrift clings in the rock clefts,
and I worry about your debts.

Water so clear, I can see gannets fishing;
air too ruthlessly pure to screen out the sun.
Innocence burns. I touch your face in my pocket
and ache with the brightness.

Saw the aurora last night; the shivering wave
of lights, of not-quite-colours too subtle to name,
drifting over the dark, like a transient smile
kindling grave eyes.

Rather

Anything rather than say
                your eyes deceived you:
that the high peak
            was never out of reach,
or that a man was less
              than your thoughts made him.
Say it the once,
         and you would always see it
that way:
        you would look out over waste acres,
never once shaping
            in rank weeds and litter
the swell of trees,
           a fountain's glittering arc,
sunflowers turning slowly,
                the scent of apples.

It's Only Love

It's just this judgement bypass; nothing drastic.
(I'm told they do it without anaesthesia.)
It leaves your conscience supple as elastic.
One of the side-effects is mild amnesia:
facts get reshaped; pain slips your mind. Some blindness
is normal. Sufferers claim to see heaven
on earth; stars in dull eyes; wit in unkindness.
This commonly resists all treatment given.
It's not all bad. Granted, no flame-retardant
will work: but still, the toxins are a tonic.
The virus leaves you selfless, brave and ardent;
anyway, once you've got the thing, it's chronic.
Most people learn to live with the condition:
what kills them is the terror of remission.

And when I got there

And when I got there,
to the far hills, the colours were tarnished
that had glowed with distance. Amethysts
faded to heather-clumps, and the green velvet
was threadbare. At the ocean's edge,
folds of radiance frayed into a scum,
frothy, discoloured, tangled with refuse,
stinking of old wrack. I have flown
through the architecture of cumulus,
and it wasn't there. And I am still looking
into dark shallows and seeing depths,
still reading poems on a blank page,
still following the perfect curve of eyebrows,
or refracted light.

The Treasure-House

Burn of Deepdale, Shetland

Nobody comes here by chance. You can't follow
this burn down its narrow, glassy banks,
and to find this one plateau, to be sitting
on a heather-clump, dropping buttercups
in the water, watching them scramble
round boulders, race to a bay of sheer rock
where boats can't land, you must clamber down
Ramna Vord, so steep you can hardly stand.
I'm looking at it now, knowing I could never
climb up again; yet Dale Hill, the way out,
is no easier: you do it without thinking
or looking down.

Since this burn named its valley; since it gouged
this cleft, it has not seen a lame man,
nor an ill, nor an old. The play of sunlight
on interlocking spurs, the brief rainbows
in waterfalls, the palette of greens,
grass, sphagnum moss, rock jade-polished
with river-slime, have been here for birds,
the odd incurious sheep, and as few
human eyes as if they were locked in a vault.
I am trailing my hand in a shock of cold,
hearing in the burn an old pirate's voice:
"*I have brought you to the treasure-house of the world.*"

Far Places

So he made it, in the end, to the top
of the west ridge; half an hour longer
by the track, while his sons went straight up
and waited for him, lounging on the heather,

laughing. He saw the mica in the rock
once more, flashing silver in the sun,
and thought, as he paused to get his breath back,
I couldn't stand not seeing it again.

And then the haul, over miles of hill
and moorland, stumbling in and out
of peat cuttings, watching his footing, while
they strode so far ahead, he couldn't shout

to them. Out of sight. He knew he'd find them
where he had led them all those years ago:
by the steep waterfall. They'd wait for him,
watching the water mist and cream and rainbow,

as mesmerised as ever. He'd rest a minute,
then scramble down beside them in the spray,
or maybe not: the view from the green height
was good enough for most folks. Either way,

it would be worth the walk, the tiredness,
to look again and feel it stop his heart.
But every distant, high, uncommon place
is getting further, harder: more effort

for the same prize. *One day,* the thought nags,
*you'll say no. Not got the lungs: too stiff.
Or it won't be the breath, the back, the legs,
but the will.* And his throat clamps with grief

for the far places: snapshots in a frame,
dim memories; a shard of silver rock
turned in the hand. The glint isn't the same
out of the sun; you never get it back.

The Garden

Outside the window is a field,
and in that field sheep graze,
backs to the wind, fleece blown forward
off their bare buttocks. Brent geese
pick around them, quicker, bright-eyed,
wide boys among the yokels. And rabbits
crop; sniff the air; drop back down;
stiffen again, living on the edge
of panic, while dapper oystercatchers
in black and white dodge between
webbed feet and cloven.

                    Open the window;
the rabbits will be a flash of white scut,
step out of doors; the oystercatchers
will take flight. As you walk toward them,
sheep back their lambs away. The geese
may front up, a hissing phalanx. They'll shuffle off,
in the end. It takes no time
to empty a field.

Ronas Hill

Red hill, granite rose
full-blown above the voe,
flooding the water's glass
with redness: mild slope swelling
so slowly, stone cumulus
in a clear sky. Crumpled fields
shadowed with green: outcrops
of bare rock blazing.

A man walking away,
his eyes still dazzled
with red, was once sunstruck
(it was June in the north: thin air,
sudden heat stooping
like a raptor). They found him
treading heather, his wits wandering
in scented eccentric circles.

Red, he slurred, over and over,
claret in a glass, autumn,
all that red in the water,
blood and fire, red: so red,
foxfur, a red mass, red
as the red planet. They cooled
his brow and soothed him, thinking
he meant the sun.

As If

Mist poured in from the sea and
never stopped, and it filled up
the dips first, and then wrapped itself
round hills, like Christo's sheets
on the Reichstag. And all Dunrossness
was whited-out, signposts
and landmarks lost, and the world
narrowed to a path, nothing
ahead nor to left nor right except
in the roadside ditches a yellow flood
of monkey-flower; as if someone
had touched off a long trail
of kerosene by design. You could see
the edge of safety, the way
to keep, by the monkey-flower
with its grinning face.

Letter

The air shattered this week: you know when the space
aches in your sinuses; the bite, the clean
bright edge of frost? Light is sharp now, the sky
bluer and farther, and when I breathe in,

my lungs drink ice. Your birthday came and went;
wind blew a drift of butterflies over
the northern isles, and the lost albatross
nested one more year without a lover.

Birds set out on their travels, same as ever:
it's nothing to them who'll miss their goodbyes,
written across the sky in small black letters
like your neat script, that will not answer this.

The Tormented Censor

He sees what is not given to others,
the foreign magazines before they are made
fit for the faithful. He makes them fit.

All day long, he sifts indecent women.
Runner's World; his glinting scissors meet
and part; amputate bare legs and arms.

All through *Hello!* his soft felt-tip is busy
stroking a chador of thick black ink
over celebrity cleavages.

Even in *Woman's Weekly*, some minx
moistens her lips with the tip of a pink tongue:
he rips it out. The whole page.

They all get shredded, the silky limbs,
the taut breasts, flesh cut to ribbons.
He is devout, and keeps none back,

but after work, walking home, if a woman
should pass, decently veiled, all in black,
his gut clenches; he tries not to look,

as the little devils in his mind whisper
what they know; melt cloth; draw curves
on her dark shapelessness.

Bryn Asaph

They are filling its name in with plaster,
the name that was incised into the stone
above its porch. Ninety years and more
in one family: now the last are gone,
an old maid and bachelor who clung on
in the old house where they were children once.
It sold in weeks. "*They* soon saw their chance",

my neighbour says, jerking his thumb
at the Home for Retired Gentlefolk.
"You wouldn't think they'd still need Lebensraum;
three huge Victorian houses.... They're in luck
now, though; they can finish off the block.
They'll have the street, one day." There's a pause.
"Hope I never end up in one of those."

You have to say they think of their visitors:
they've paved the old garden, so the frail
and crippled can be parked at the very doors;
they've knocked a space in that low stone wall
out front, for when ambulances call
in the night. Now their colours, white and grey,
advance over the new territory,

blending it in.... Sometimes I see young nurses
wheeling a batch of inmates to the park,
blanketed, shapeless. The cracked whiskery faces
are hard to read: they don't always look
female or male. I can't tell if they like
going out; if they'd rather be elsewhere;
if anyone consults them. They don't live here,

as people do who plant daffodils, choose
the colours of curtains; when to go in or out.
Workmen are bricking up the side windows
of what was once Bryn Asaph: sad, that,
like putting out its eyes, but sadder yet
the name gone from the stone, the smooth surface
that says: *Before this, nothing was.*

There was such a house: its name was Bryn Asaph,
it stood in such a road, in such a city,
through the twentieth century, near enough,
and all that time home to one family.
In 'ninety-seven, its singularity
and past were plastered over: it became
no-one's home, with no story and no name.

Aardvark

so it's Sunday afternoon at Mum's,
and I'm dozing off, and she asks: *how's Mo?*
meaning *where's Mo*, and I say: *busy,
very busy*, and her lips tighten,
and I'm sentenced to the photographs
of my cousin's wedding.

And I go *mm* at the right moments,
and wish I was home, moaning at Mo.
Families.... My sister's kid is watching
wildlife eat each other on the box,
when a word leaps out and makes him laugh.
Aardvark. I come awake,

like someone sent a few volts through me,
and try to breathe easy. Think wedding groups;
think posies. But the kid can't let it go.
Aardvark, aardvark; through helpless giggles,
wiping tears, holding his aching ribs.
My face feels hot.

When *no; please don't* and *stop* are stripped
of their meanings, you need another word,
your word, to say all that. One you'd not use
in the normal way; one you can't mistake
when you hear it screamed or sobbed. It only
needs saying once,

and the pain stops. He's wheezing now,
hysterical, and it's like my worst dream;
Mo smiling, twisting cord, stroking the edge
of metal across flesh, and me gasping
over and over: *aardvark, aardvark, aardvark*,
and it doesn't stop....

The City of Empty Rooms

There's a city above the city, above street level,
above the blankets wheezing in doorways,
above the window-dressers' tableaux
and the "sale" signs; above the gold lettering
of the third-floor solicitors, higher yet,

the city of empty rooms. They're carpeted
in deep-pile dust, wall-to-wall silence,
cavity isolation. *Secluded residence
commanding extensive views. No parking.*
Pollsters and canvassers don't climb this far;

no census-takers nor rent collectors.
The city in the air was never surveyed,
the *Rough Guide* missed it out; no-one has studied
its population, its mythology.
Up there, anything might be possible:

maybe the hidden roof-slopes are covered
in gardens; maybe the empty rooms are there
for those who need them, and the gentle murmur
from all the eaves: *loving, loving, loving,*
is the voice not of pigeons but of doves.

Pause: Rewind

Nowadays the dead walk and talk
in the wedding video, the camcorded break,

the fuzzed black-and-white of security cameras.
A policeman watches, as two balaclavas

burst, again and again, through the door
of an off-licence, and the old shopkeeper

panics: blunders into a baseball bat;
slumps in his blood. Before things can get

any worse, the young D.C. presses "pause",
then "rewind". And the dark stream flows

into the head again: the old fellow
gets up: the thieves are backing jerkily through

the door, which closes on them. All right;
all tidy. This could get to be a habit:

so many tapes he could whizz backwards.
That bus and bike, speeding to the crossroads,

will not collide: the drunk at the hotel
will stop short of his car: the young girl

will never disappear down the subway
where her rapist waits so patiently.

Pause: rewind. Freeze-frame where you want
the world to stop. The moment before the moment;

before Challenger leaves the launch pad,
before the boat sails or the letter's posted,

before the singer jumps off the bridge,
before you see the face that ends your marriage,

before the pink suit is dyed red,
before a thought is formed or a word said.

Unkindness

A dead man is so like to a man sleeping,
whispered the professor, when she laid eyes
on the gentle face a peat-spade turned over
in Tollund bog. The centuries-old unkindness

that buried him there had only marked his brow
with little furrows, like a man's in a dream.
He lay relaxed on his side. She almost thought
she could have shaken his shoulder and woken him.

So I feel, seeing you lie, somewhat stiffer
than usual, so that lifting your slight weight
is no such easy matter. I can't notice
anything missing: no, not even the light

of wit in your open eyes. There is just the stiffness,
and a little crust of dried blood at the mouth,
and is that any reason to leave a kind companion
alone for an iron age in the black earth?

Crossing the Bridge

He was on his way
to buy a wedding ring,
singing as he went.

Crossing Cardiff Bridge,
he met his old love,
and they fell in talk;

she wished him joy
of his wedding, and said
it was fine weather

for the time of year,
and his whole heart
went out to her.

Between water and air,
country and town,
the world alters:

not here but there,
not Elizabeth but Joan,
not what I thought,

but what surprised me.
He stood on a bridge
and let it happen,

or made it happen:
who knows how
these bridges work,

though we stand so often
on a stone moment,
an arc of choice,

or chance. Sometimes
we are Joan, the mover,
the change in the air;

sometimes the left-behind,
so much Elizabeth
under the bridge;

sometimes the man
in the middle, transfixed
by a shining word,

sun on his face,
the sweet certainty
that crossing the bridge

will change everything
for better or worse,
and he can't go back.

Note: From an incident recounted by William Thomas in his Diaries, 1762-1795, pub. The Cardiff South Wales Record Society, 1995. Harry Edward went to buy the ring for his wedding to Elizabeth Water. Crossing the bridge into Cardiff, he met his old love Joan Morgan, and before he was over the bridge had decided to marry her instead, which he did.

The Comet-Watcher's Perspective

Granted, it was a streak of cobalt ice
a million miles across; it came from the edge
of creation, once in a thousand years,
but look as he might, it was just a blue smudge.

This is small, but that is far away:
there's a face, a silver stud in a pointed chin,
black hair, brown eyes, that he can no more hold
with his, than he could stare into the sun.

Tutorial

I know: the words came flooding into your head,
and you just wrote them down.... Now look again;
work out what you really wanted to say,
and how you failed to say it. Then you can.

And yes, some of it works. So concentrate
on what doesn't. And when *that* takes off,
go back to what you thought were the good bits
and craft them better. Good's not good enough.

Play with the line. Turn it around, and see
what happens. Try taking a stress away;
change tense, loosen the rhythm. Shake the words up
like patterns in a kaleidoscope. Just play.

Climb into someone else's story,
think in his voice, bring him alive, move on
to the next. Become a vent act, a shape-changer.
Why settle for just you? Be everyone.

Open up: look and listen so hard,
it hurts. Taste the frost on the air,
the blood on your tongue. Half-alive is too dull
for words; will make no mark on blank paper.

Argue back. Tell me I'm wrong. I've been doing
the same tricks for years: make me learn,
surprise me. Take a word for a walk
down a new road where I have never been.

Take your gift and polish it; make it shine
bright enough for praise, too bright for jealousy.
The best work any artist can leave
is a pupil who outshines him. Go beyond me.

TRANSLATIONS

SIMON DACH (1605-1659)

Perstet amicitiae semper venerabile Faedus!
(May the bond of friendship always be held in honour)

What so adorns our being;
what fits a human so,
as making friends and staying
true to our friendship's vow;
when with our fellow-creature
we enter in a bond
sealed with our human nature,
upheld by word and hand?

If speech is purely human,
then humans must be born
to live their lives in common,
not separate and alone.
We should consult, and borrow
each other's wits at need,
and talk about the sorrow
that no-one can avoid.

What is the use of laughter
upon the empty wind?
A joke is funny, after
you share it with a friend.
And he who pours his grief out
shall by and by find ease,
but he will fret his life out
who hugs his trouble close.

If my love's first direction
is God, that man must be
the next in my affection
who shares himself with me.

With these my sworn companions
I can face pain and smile,
harrow hell's deepest canyons
and break death's prison cell.

I have such friends; true-minded
as could be asked of men;
whose love is not pretended,
nor given in mocking vein.
I prize them too, these others
rooted so deep in me.
I love you more, my brothers,
than all earth's treasury.

ANDREAS GRYPHIUS (1616-1664)

Mittag
(Midday)

Come, friends, and eat. The sun will not remain
so high for long, cleaving his element,
breaking our day, before his long descent
sets the heat-weary world to work again.
His flaming arrows spread a scorching stain
across the flowers; the field, all moisture spent,
longs for the dew; the reaper for the tent,
and not one bird sings of its loving pain.
Now the light rules. Black shadows shrink, and keep
to holes and corners, as a man may creep
who, out of shame or fear, must hide his face.
We surely may escape the noonday's glare,
but not that other light which everywhere
sees us and weighs us, piercing each dark place.

CHRISTIAN HOFMANN VON HOFMANNSWALDAU (1617-1679)

An Floriden
(To Fleur)

The other day, my tortured mind was reeling,
my eyes were full of fire and water both.
I longed to pour out all that I was feeling,
but I was choked for spirit and for breath.
I scanned the heaven that sent my sufferings,
and then the virgin star whose slave I am,
and though I wished to say a thousand things,
in the end there is nothing but this rhyme.
I am a chaste heart fired by chastity,
whom fashion and appearance could not move,
who sets his hope upon your purity
and lays his whole soul at your feet in love.
I know that love-talk isn't to your taste,
because it leads to folly, and I swear
that as I would not love someone unchaste,
so I would never wish to lead you there.
I love no ornament; no silk can please me:
it is the work of worms, and their food too.
It takes more than fine costume to amaze me;
I have seen gold and pearls: they're nothing new.
It was your guileless speech that caught my mind,
your unmalicious fun that chained my heart.
You are so lovable, so simply kind,
that I wish we might never be apart.
Consider: can a flame you lit be other
than pure, like you? I promise faithfully,
if you let thoughts and kisses come together,
that I will be your match in chastity:
I swear a kiss is where my longing ends.
I'll write no more: I need sleep now, to stop
the storm in me. I kiss your fleece-white hands
and end this verse, but not, I hope, my hope.

PAUL FLEMING (1609-1640)

Für eine Jungfrau
(For a young lady, to send to her sweetheart)

The month of May is coming,
her pretty cheeks all blooming,
the flowers in her face.
The frost's long grief unfreezes
with the warm western breezes,
and pleasure takes its place.

And love too will be dawning;
will put off winter's mourning
and smile bright as the sun.
And all our senses call us;
the whole world seems to tell us:
Let those who love be one.

This ribbon that I send you,
let it adorn and bind you:
it's fit I make you fine.
Oh all my longings, reach him,
and put it on him; touch him.
I wish your luck were mine.

May God lay on my lover
as many marks of favour
as stars in heaven may be;
as twigs are in the hedgerows,
as grasses in the meadows,
as fish swim in the sea.

Auf das Gedächtnis seiner ersten Freundin
(On remembering his first girlfriend*)

Though I must let her go, I am hers yet,
and she is mine, whatever comes between.
Things happen: life doles out pleasure and pain
at its own liking. I will try to put
a brave face on; be gracious, as is fit.
Image of good, she is and is not mine,
that pretty child. If I found hate within
my heart for her, I'd hate myself for it.
You take her, Fate: don't worry about me.
Kidnap her body, yet her soul will be
a part of mine, however far apart.
Oh my soul's light, the best of you won't go
from me, and though, my joy, I can't have you,
the thought of you will always lift my heart.

Who had left him, and married another man.

Auf ihre Gesundheit
(For her sake)

Every sleeping, waking hour,
every dream of every night,
every time I act or wait,
all I want and all I fear,
every laugh and every tear,
all I drink and all I eat,
all I think and read and write,
this and that and so much more,
all I don't do; all I do,
pain and pleasure, joy and sorrow,
every time I rest or move,
all and nothing: all of this,
every day, for all my days,
for the sake of one I love.

CHRISTINE DE PISAN (1363-1430s)

Se souvent vais au moustier
(If I'm in church every day)

If I'm in church every day,
it's all to watch that young face
open like a new rose.

There is nothing to say:
why should it make news
if I'm in church every day?

I walk no path and no way
for any other cause.
Fools: call me fool as you please,
if I'm in church every day.

Le plus bel des fleurs de lys
(Of all the lilies of the field)

> Of all the lilies of the field
> fairest, worthiest of praise,
> at my will in all ways,
> my choice, unparalleled.
>
> Young, beautiful and mild
> of manner: my courteous prize
> of all the lilies of the field.
>
> And if I bloom, fulfilled
> in his love; if he is
> my all, blame me the less
> that it was him I chose and held
> of all the lilies of the field.

De triste cuer chanter joyeusement
(To sing a happy song with a sad heart)

> To sing a happy song with a sad heart,
> to feel one thing and fake the contrary,
> to coax a light laugh out of misery;
> no actor ever played a harder part,
>
> but I must do so: it is what I've taught
> myself. This is my only remedy;
> to sing a happy song with a sad heart,
>
> for what would I be otherwise but sport,
> in love with one who does not care for me?
> I will hide pain in smiles, sooner than be
> the common talk. It is a bitter art
> to sing a happy song with a sad heart.

Notes

I've avoided footnotes for years, not because I dislike them but because reviewers inevitably do. Some readers do too; others — like me — would sometimes welcome them. So I have put these at the back, where they won't get in the way of the poems and where readers who want to ignore them can.

'The Arctic Chart': Parry was an early seeker for the North-West Passage; *Fury* was one of his ships. Kane, Bellot and M'Clintock were all involved in the "Great Search" for the missing Franklin expedition in the 1840s and 50s. Bellot (diminutive only in physical terms) and M'Clintock went out as unpaid freelances on ships financed by Lady Franklin, who, unlike the Admiralty, refused to give up her search for the missing men until the unstoppable M'Clintock found their remains.

'Envying Owen Beattie': I feel I should stress that this is factual up to line 31, after which it falls into the category of "what I'd have done if it were me". It isn't meant to imply that the real Beattie, the archaeologist, actually kissed the dead face resting on his shoulder — merely that in his place, I couldn't have resisted doing so.

'Pause: Rewind:' The "drunk at the hotel" is not meant to be the unfortunate M. Henri Paul. I wrote the poem before Diana's death and it has nothing to do with her — its immediate inspiration was an episode of *The Bill*, plus some personal reminiscences. The "pink suit" of the last verse was worn by Jacqueline Kennedy in Dallas. A quick poll of my students suggests that hardly anyone under fifty knows that now, but to me and some of my contemporaries it was an unforgettable image and sometimes you have to risk being generation-specific.

Acknowledgements

Some of these poems and translations have previously appeared in *BABEL, The Bridport Competition Anthology 1997, Dove-Marks on Stone: Poems for George Mackay Brown* (Babel, 1997), *The Exeter Poetry Prize Anthology 1998, The Forward Book of Poetry 1999, The Interpreter's House, The New Orleans Review, The New Welsh Review, The North, Obsessed with Pipework, Planet, Poetry Life, Poetry Review, Poetry Wales, Soundings, Thumbscrew* and *The Yellow Crane*.

'Envying Owen Beattie' was a finalist in the Cardiff International Poetry Competition and the winner of the Forward Poetry Prize for the best poem of 1998.

'Crossing the Bridge' was joint winner in the Bridport Competition for 1997.

'Far Places' was a finalist in the Exeter Poetry Competition for 1998.